Judges 1-8

THE SPIRAL OF FAITH

CWR

Phin Hall

Published 2012 by CWR, Waverley Abbey House, Waverley Lane, Farnham, Surrey GU9 8EP, UK. Registered Charity No. 294387. Registered Limited Company No. 1990308.

See back of book for list of National Distributors.

Unless otherwise indicated, all Scripture references are from the Holy Bible: New International Version (NIV), copyright © 1973, 1978, 1984 by the International Bible Society.

Concept development, editing, design and production by CWR

Cover image: istock/Nikola Spasenoski

Printed in the UK by Page Brothers

ISBN: 978-1-85345-681-7

Contents

Introduction

'Why on earth are we studying this horrible book?'

This was a genuine question asked by a church member faced with a series on Judges, and while the obvious response is 'Because it is in the Bible', it is actually a fair question. The book of Judges tells the story of one of the darker periods in Israelite history, and as such it contains a number of things that can be hard to read, though all too easy to imagine. People's guts are spilled out, nails are hammered through heads, bodies are hacked to pieces and then mailed around the country, and so on. The narrator certainly makes no attempt to cover up the gory details of the reign of these judges.

The title 'judge' is a curious one, as the role did not involve wearing wigs or presiding over a courtroom as the term implies today. A more accurate title might be 'saviour', 'deliverer' or even 'warlord', since the main task of the judges was to go to war against the enemies of Israel.

In total there are six main judges – Othniel, Ehud, Deborah (who, together with Barak and Jael, counts as one), Gideon, Jephthah and Samson – plus another six minor judges. Considering this book nestles between the time of Joshua and the birth of Samuel – a period of roughly 300 years – this begs the question: 'Why were there so many judges?'

The simple answer is that Israel needed them, because they kept getting caught in a cycle of events. This cycle is detailed in the second chapter of Judges, and followed this pattern:
• The Israelites worshipped idols instead of God;
• God allowed a foreign nation to oppress them;
• They cried out to God, and so He raised up a judge to deliver them;

- The Israelites worshipped idols instead of God, and so on.

Six accounts of this cycle are given in Judges, and far from learning their lesson, the Israelites get progressively worse as the cycles unfold. The book of Judges is, therefore, more an account of Israel's downward spiral than simply a repeated cycle of events.

It opens with two introductions – the first being an account of events 'on the ground', and the second being more of an overview, giving the background to these events and a preview of coming attractions. The accounts of the judges then start with the exemplary reign of Othniel, but it is all downhill from there, and this study guide closes with the sad story of how Gideon's faith failed, and he led all Israel astray.

So, faced with the gory details, the downward spiral of Israel, and the prospect of an unhappy ending, the question of why to study Judges remains.

In 1 Corinthians 10, Paul gives us our reason. Writing about the troubled times of Israel's past, he said, 'These things happened to them as examples and were written down as warnings for us, on whom the fulfilment of the ages has come' (v.11). Even in the midst of the brutality and the bloodshed, God is speaking to us through His Word; teaching and warning us.

As we work our way through the warfare, and look beyond the bad behaviour, we will discover a book that is all about faith. In these first eight chapters of the book of Judges, we are taught:

- *The importance of faith*. God places such a high value on it that our eternal future is decided on our faith (or lack of it)! We will look at what faith is, and why it is so vital.

- *What can be achieved when, in faith, we work together with God.* This is one of the great privileges of being a child of God, and we will see not only what we can accomplish, but just how little else we need besides our faith.
- *How faith is demonstrated through the way we live.* As James points out, 'Faith by itself, if it is not accompanied by action, is dead' (James 2:17). We will consider the link between faith and deeds, and how this applies to our everyday lives.
- *God's commitment to growing and shaping our faith.* Since our faith is so important to God, He is not content that it should be static, and instead He works to increase our faith. We will identify several ways in which God achieves this, some of which are less comfortable for us than others.

In addition to this, our voyage through these first chapters will also warn us of those things that can damage our faith in God, and draw us away from keeping Him at the centre of our lives. When you think of all it has in store for us, surely this 'horrible book' is worth our time and our attention!

You will get the most out of these studies if you take the time to read through the complete passage assigned to each session before you start working through the Discussion Starters. Some of these passages are fairly long, but be encouraged, they are worth the effort.

Our prayer is that, as you use this study guide, and work your way through these first, exciting chapters of Judges, you will find your own faith being grown and shaped by God. And be assured, your faith is 'of greater worth than gold' (1 Pet. 1:7)!

WEEK 1

Land Not Taken

Opening Icebreaker

Go round the group with each person saying one 'everyday' thing they believe to be true and how this is shown by what they do. For example, 'I believe the Royal Mail will deliver my parcel, so I will take it to the Post Office' or 'I believe that exercise is good for me, so I walk to work … sometimes.'

Bible Readings

- Judges 1:1–2:5 (if short of time just read Judges 1:1–8 and 27–34)
- Deuteronomy 7:1–6
- Hebrew 5:7–9
- James 2:14–20

Key Verse: 'The LORD was with the men of Judah. They took possession of the hill country, but they were unable to drive the people from the plains, because they had iron chariots.' (1:19)

Focus: Faith is of great importance to God, and our faith is shown by our actions.

Opening Our Eyes

The book of Judges opens on the brink of war – a fitting start as the Israelites spend most of this book in conflicts of one kind or another. They were about to go up against the Canaanites, the current inhabitants of the promised land, and so they asked the Lord which tribe should go to battle first. He replied, 'Judah is to go; I have given the land into their hands' (1:2).

So with this promise to spur them on, Judah went to war, and at first things went well. They defeated the cities of Bezek and Jerusalem, the hill country and the Negev (the southern area of the land). City after city fell before them, and they destroyed one settlement so completely that they renamed it 'Hormah', a term which implies total destruction!

Sadly, in verse 19, the wave of victories come to an end. This verse begins by reminding us that these triumphs were God-given – 'The LORD was with the men of Judah' – but then comes the defeat: 'They took possession of the hill country, but they were unable to drive the people from the plains, because they had iron chariots.' The Lord had *promised* to give the Canaanites into their hands, but when they were faced with this superior military machine Judah's faith failed, and they advanced no further.

From this point on, it went downhill for the Israelites. 'The Benjamites ... failed to dislodge the Jebusites' (v.21). 'Manasseh did not drive out the people of Beth Shan' (v.27) and a number of other settlements. 'Nor did Ephraim drive out the Canaanites living in Gezer' (v.29). 'Neither did Zebulun drive out the Canaanites' (v.30). 'Nor did Asher drive out those living in Acco' (v.31) and six other cities. 'Neither did Naphtali drive out those living in Beth Shemesh' (v.33).

Worst of all was the tribe of Dan who, far from driving out the Amorites, were instead forced by them to live in the hills! Chapter 1 then ends with a description of the land held by these Amorites, and the phrasing used by the narrator is a clear mockery of the tribal allotments given in Joshua (eg Josh. 15).

Can you imagine it? Here was this vast expanse of land that had been promised them by God, and yet the Israelites had to squeeze themselves in among the Canaanites in only a fraction of it. It is a sad record of the failure of the Israelites to take their tribal allotments. And yet, this was the promised land, the land which God said He would give them. Surely, then, the fault did not lie entirely with Israel. Was God not able to deliver on His promise? Had He failed them?

The message from the angel of the Lord in chapter 2 clears up any confusion over this matter. Yes, God had promised to give them the land, but the Israelites had disobeyed Him. They had compromised, they had failed to destroy their enemies and they had demonstrated a lack of faith in God's promise. This was why they failed to receive what was promised.

Instead, in verse 3, the angel lays the foundation for the downward spiral that makes up the rest of this book: 'Now therefore I tell you that I will not drive them out before you; they will be thorns in your sides and their gods will be a snare to you.'

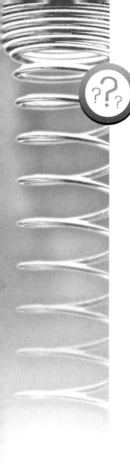

Discussion Starters

1. When you read the excuses for the Israelites not taking the land (Judg. 1:19,27,34), how reasonable do you consider them to be?

2. God had commanded the Israelites, in Deuteronomy 7:2, to destroy the inhabitants without mercy. Read the short asides in Judges 1:5–7 and 23–26. How do these stories line up with God's command?

3. R.T. Kendall defined faith as 'believing God', and James 2:17 tells us that 'faith by itself, if it is not accompanied by action, is dead'. Can you think of examples either in the Bible or in your own life where believing God is shown through people's actions?

4. God could have driven out the Canaanites in an instant, yet He wanted the Israelites to act in faith. Why do you think faith is so important to God?

_____

_____

_____

_____

_____

5. The Israelites failed to take the land because they did not believe God's promise that He would drive out the inhabitants. Why do you think their faith failed them?

_____

_____

_____

_____

_____

6. Consider some of the great promises from God, such as John 3:16, Romans 8:28, 1 John 1:9 and Revelation 22:12. Does your faith in these promises affect the way you live and, if so, how?

_____

_____

_____

_____

_____

7. The result of the Israelites' faithless disobedience was that they lost the promise from God to drive out the Canaanites. Do you think Christians can ever miss out on God's promises in such a way?

_____

_____

_____

_____

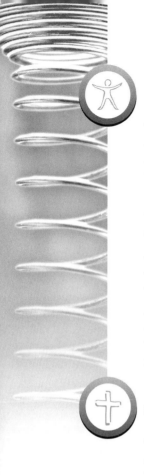

Personal Application

The taking of the promised land is often seen as a picture of the believer's progress to maturity in Christ, as sin is driven out and God's rule spreads to all areas of our lives. Like the Israelites, God has given us many promises, such as: 'His divine power has given us everything we need for life and godliness' (2 Pet. 1:3); and '… he who began a good work in you will carry it on to completion' (Phil. 1:6).

Though God could make us perfect the instant we believe, He wants us to work together with Him, believing in His promises and so seeing them fulfilled. As we begin our voyage through Judges, we need to consider this choice: Will we believe God and work together with Him, or will we be like the Israelites whose faith failed them in the face of opposition and hardship?

Seeing Jesus in the Scriptures

The writer to the Hebrews tells us that Jesus 'learned obedience' (5:8), remaining faithful to God's will despite being subject to human frailty.

Jesus is our great example of faithful obedience, because He looked to God for guidance at every moment. Every miracle performed, every word spoken, every step taken was done in faith. If we are ever uncertain about the value of faith, we need only look to Jesus. He demonstrated absolute faith in God, and the result of His faithful obedience is that we can be forgiven for our faithless disobedience, becoming children of God, with the hope that one day we will take our heavenly promised land!

WEEK 2

The Shape of Things to Come

Opening Icebreaker

Go round the group sharing either one thing you have been taught about God in the last month, or who the first person was to tell to you about Jesus.

Bible Readings

- Judges 2:6–3:6 (if short of time just read Judges 2:10–19)
- Leviticus 10:11
- Deuteronomy 4:9–14; 6:6–9
- Matthew 28:19–20
- Romans 10:14

Key Verse: 'After that whole generation had been gathered to their fathers, another generation grew up, who knew neither the LORD nor what he had done for Israel.' (2:10)

Focus: To ensure faith continues to spread, we must teach the next generation the truth about God.

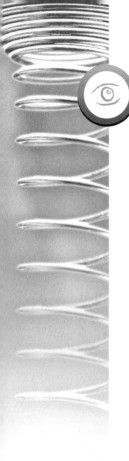

Opening Our Eyes

While there are those who enjoy the detective novel that keeps you guessing to the end, there are others who prefer it when the crime and its perpetrator are revealed in the opening chapter. There is something about knowing 'whodunit' that intensifies the story and heightens the suspense, and in this second introduction to the book of Judges, the narrator does just this by revealing to us the shape of things to come.

Verses 11–19 detail the cycle that we will see repeated six times in this book:
• The Israelites do evil in the eyes of the Lord, worshipping idols instead of Him.
• God responds by giving them over to an enemy, who oppresses them until the Israelites cry out for God to save them.
• The Lord raises up a judge to deliver them from their oppressor, but once they have been freed the Israelites soon go back to doing evil again.

Looking at this cycle one cannot help wondering why the Israelites kept getting caught in this depressing sequence of events. Verse 10 gives us the answer: '... another generation grew up, who knew neither the LORD nor what he had done for Israel.' Each cycle began because one generation failed to teach the next the truth about God.

We saw in the previous session how important faith is, and to ensure that it continued to spread, God gave clear responsibility for teaching the people to the priests (Lev. 10) and to parents: '... do not forget the things your eyes have seen or let them slip from your heart as long as you live. Teach them to your children and to their children after them' (Deut. 4:9). The priests and parents were to teach the people about all God had done for them, and so the repeated cycle we see throughout

Judges was the direct result of their failure to do so. Amazingly it only took a single generation after the death of Joshua for the first cycle to begin!

Since they were not taught the truth about God, the Israelites forgot Him and instead they 'served the Baals' (Judg. 2:11). These were various fertility gods that the Canaanite peoples worshipped, often in the form of idols made of wood or stone. Though worshipping such handmade deities may seem foolish to us, the people of the ancient world believed that if you served these gods then the rains would come, your crops would not fail, your flocks would increase and your family would prosper. You can imagine how attractive this would have seemed, and so it is really not surprising that when the Israelites were not taught about the one, true God, they were quickly drawn in by these Baals.

All, however, was not lost, and though the priests and parents had failed in their responsibility, God used the situation to teach them Himself. He used the nations that remained '… to test Israel and see whether they will keep the way of the Lord' (2:22). He used them '… to teach warfare to the descendants of the Israelites who had not had previous battle experience' (3:2). And we shall see that He also used them to cause Israel to turn to God and cry out to Him.

Regardless of how we feel about warfare, it is still great to know that, though the Israelites were delinquent in their duties, God still watched over them. He would not allow their faith to die out completely.

Discussion Starters

1. Why did the Israelites keep falling into the cycle that is revealed in this chapter? Does it surprise you?

    _____

    _____

    _____

    _____

2. What do you see as being God's main purpose in taking His people through these cycles?

    _____

    _____

    _____

    _____

3. Through these cycles, God allowed His people to suffer in order to teach them and bring them back to faith in Him. Do you believe God still uses suffering and hardship in this way today?

    _____

    _____

    _____

    _____

4. Read Leviticus 10:11, Deuteronomy 4:9–14 and 6:6–9. The Israelites clearly failed in their task. What might have kept the Israelites from keeping these commands to pass on the truth about God to the next generation?

    _____

    _____

    _____

    _____

5. The 'next generation' today may be thought of not only as our children, but as all those who do not know God. Whose responsibility is it to pass on the truth about Him to this 'next generation'? (See also Matthew 28:19–20.)

_____

_____

_____

_____

_____

6. What might keep _us_ from passing on the truth about God to the 'next generation'?

_____

_____

_____

_____

_____

7. With the promise of prosperity, the Baals drew Israel away from worshipping the Lord to serving idols instead. We will look more at idols in week 7, but for now discuss how worldly prosperity can affect our own faith in God.

_____

_____

_____

_____

_____

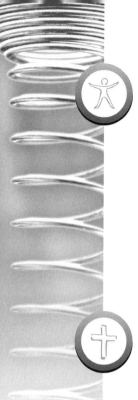

Personal Application

The next generation of believers is all around us. They are in our towns and cities, our workplaces and colleges, even our homes. When considering all those who had yet to call on the Lord and be saved, Paul said, 'How, then, can they call on the one they have not believed in? And how can they believe in the one of whom they have not heard? And how can they hear without someone preaching to them?' (Rom. 10:14). We saw in the last session that our faith is shown by our actions. Do our lives show that we really believe we are called to pass on the truth about God to the next generation?

Seeing Jesus in the Scriptures

The opening chapter of Mark's Gospel barely pauses for breath in its all-action account of the beginning of Jesus' ministry. The first character we see is John the Baptist, calling the people to repentance. Then, no sooner has Jesus been baptised and John arrested, than we see Jesus continuing this work of preaching the gospel: 'The kingdom of God is near. Repent and believe the good news!' (Mark 1:15). Arguably the greatest part of Jesus' ministry was teaching the next generation about God and the kingdom.

Before Jesus ascended into heaven, He passed on the responsibility to His followers. 'Therefore go and make disciples of all nations, baptising them in the name of the Father and of the Son and of the Holy Spirit, and teaching them to obey everything I have commanded you' (Matt. 28:19–20).

WEEK 3

Othniel: the Foremost Judge

Opening Icebreaker

Ask each member of the group what their favourite game or sport is. Chat about the pros and cons of those which are team games (such as football, volleyball and bridge) versus those which are singles' games (such as tennis, karting and chess).

Bible Readings

- Judges 3:7–11
- Judges 1:11–15
- Luke 4:16–21
- John 5:19
- Galatians 5:16–18,25

Key Verse: 'But when they cried out to the LORD, he raised up for them a deliverer, Othniel son of Kenaz, Caleb's younger brother, who saved them.' (3:9)

Focus: Our faith is most effective when we work together with God in the power of His Spirit.

Opening Our Eyes

Finally, in chapter 3, we meet the first of our judges: Othniel. Actually, we have already met him back in chapter 1. He was Caleb's younger brother, the one who took Kiriath Sepher and won the hand of Acsah. When you consider that Othniel was part of the generation that fought under Joshua, it is amazing to think that during his lifetime the people of Israel forgot about the Lord and all He had done, and turned instead to worship idols. Othniel, however, had not forgotten, because he had seen many of God's great deeds with his own eyes.

As per the cycle we saw in the last session, the Israelites' unfaithfulness led to God handing them over to the first of Israel's oppressors, Cushan-Rishathaim. This was almost certainly not his real name, since it means 'dark double-evil' and even the people of the ancient world did not bestow such names on their newborn children! However, by giving him this impressive mouthful of a name, the narrator is conjuring up a terrifying figure that should strike fear into the hearts of his readers.

This Cushan came from Aram, in northwest Mesopotamia (if you have a map showing Abraham's journeys in the back of your Bible, Haran is in the middle of the Aram region). This means Cushan travelled the furthest to oppress the Israelites. As such, this dark, double-evil king is often assumed to have been the worst of the oppressors in this book, even though his tyranny lasted only eight years. And against this great enemy, as His people cried out to be saved, God raised up Othniel.

It is worth noting the literary beauty of this passage. In the Hebrew text, these fives verses are composed of eight lines before and after a single word. In the first eight we have Israel plunging into despair: they did evil; they forgot the Lord; they served idols; they roused the Lord to anger; they were given into the hands of Cushan; they served him for eight years; they cried out to the Lord; He raised up a deliverer. In the final eight we see the complete reversal of Israel's downfall: we have Othniel, Caleb's brother; he was filled with the Spirit; he judged Israel; he went to war; Cushan was given into his hands; Othniel overpowered him; the land had peace for forty years; Othniel's life and reign came to an end.

At the heart of these sixteen lines is the word translated, 'he saved them'. And this may seem insignificant, until you realise that the author of this salvation is deliberately ambiguous – in context it could refer either to the Lord or to Othniel.

So who was it? Who saved the Israelites from this terrible oppressor? The answer is, of course, they both did. As already shown in chapter 1, Othniel was a man of great bravery and faith, and now, when he was filled with the Spirit, he and God worked as one, fully identified together as they saved Israel.

Of all the major judges in this book, Othniel is the only one who fulfils every stage of the cycle as detailed in the last session. In his account alone there is no room for criticism. As our first judge, Othniel is presented as the foremost – the paragon against whom all others must be measured.

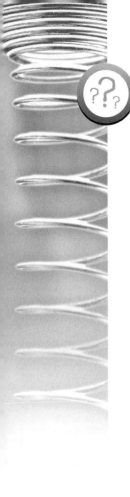

Discussion Starters

1. What strikes you most in the short account of Othniel's reign as judge?

_____

_____

_____

_____

2. The phrase 'sold ... into the hands' (v.8) refers to someone being completely given over to the mercy, or lack of mercy, of another. What was God's purpose in such harsh treatment, and was it effective?

_____

_____

_____

_____

3. When the Israelites cried out to God, He acted on their behalf. Have you ever experienced such a response from God in your own life?

_____

_____

_____

_____

4. Why do you think God chose Othniel to be the first of the judges?

_____

_____

_____

_____

5. What do you understand by the phrase 'the Spirit of the LORD came upon him' (v.10)?

_____

_____

_____

_____

_____

6. Read Galatians 5:16–18,25. What does it mean to 'keep in step with the Spirit', and how does this work out in practice?

_____

_____

_____

_____

_____

7. By faith, the Spirit-filled Othniel worked in unison with God, and so carried out a complete reversal of the situation in Israel – eight years of oppression became forty years of peace. How does this affect your own faith and desire to keep in step with the Spirit?

_____

_____

_____

_____

_____

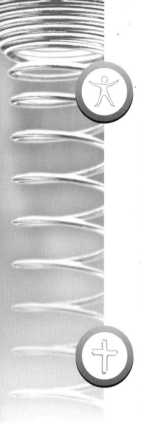

Personal Application

Othniel was used mightily by God, because he had faith and was empowered by the Holy Spirit. As God's children we are called to be different and to make a difference. The great news is that we are not expected to do this alone. Again and again we are told that the same Spirit that filled Othniel lives in us (eg Rom. 8:11; 2 Cor. 1:22 and 1 John 4:13).

Just like Othniel, we need to act in faith, keeping in step with the Holy Spirit as He guides and leads us. Can you imagine the difference you could make if you followed Othniel's example of how to work together with God?

Seeing Jesus in the Scriptures

There are a number of clear parallels between the story of Othniel and the ministry of Jesus:
• The Spirit of the Lord empowered them both (see Luke 4:16–21).
• In each of them we see both man and God working together for salvation!
• A complete reversal of evil for good was accomplished through both – Jesus reversing the evil that began at the Fall.

In John 5, speaking about His ministry, Jesus made this amazing statement: 'I tell you the truth, the Son can do nothing by himself; he can do only what he sees his Father doing, because whatever the Father does the Son also does' (v.19). Like Othniel, Jesus worked together with God. All He achieved was done in perfect partnership with the Father, and together they accomplished the greatest feat in history!

WEEK 4

Ehud: A Man with a Message

Opening Icebreaker

Household objects are usually designed with a specific purpose in mind, but most could be put to other uses. A hat could be used as a flowerpot, or a towel as an impromptu parachute (though this is not recommended as an alternative to stairs or ladders!). Go round the group thinking of other household objects and the 'alternative' uses to which they could be put.

Bible Readings

- Judges 3:12–31
- 1 Samuel 16:1–4
- 1 Corinthians 10:31
- 1 Peter 4:10

Key Verse: 'I have a secret message for you, O king.' (3:19)

Focus: God uses people of faith wherever they are, with whatever they have, to do His work.

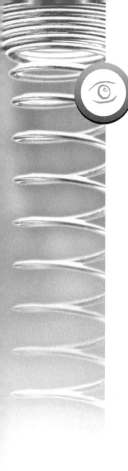

Opening Our Eyes

In contrast to the sparse account of Othniel, the story of our second judge is full of detail – even of the most gruesome and gory kind. This time, when the Israelites started worshipping idols, God handed them over to the Moabites. Though related to Israel, the Moabites attacked them, setting up their headquarters in Jericho, 'the City of Palms', and in came their king, Eglon, who is diplomatically described as 'a very fat man' (v.17). After eighteen years of oppression Israel finally cried out to the Lord, who raised up a somewhat enigmatic judge. On the one hand, Ehud is clearly a great man of faith. Yet on the other he is also a devious trickster.

Ehud was tasked with taking a tribute from the Israelites to Eglon – as was the custom – and having completed this duty, he and his companions headed back home. After only a few miles, however, Ehud turned back to visit Eglon alone. And so the trickery begins ... 'I have a secret message for you, O king,' said Ehud (v.19) – a statement which could also be translated, 'I have a secret thing for you'. The 'thing' in question was a homemade dagger – long enough to kill, yet short enough to be concealed under his clothing. This is the first of a series of makeshift weapons in this book. In verse 31 Shamgar slayed Philistines with an oxgoad, and later we will see Jael's use of a tent peg and Samson's use of a donkey's jawbone – each one making use of what they had to hand.

It is suggested that Ehud sneaked his dagger past the guards because he was left-handed and so wore it not on the left as usual, but on his right. We cannot be sure whether this is true, but it certainly suggests a rather complacent attitude to security on the part of the Moabites! And so Ehud smuggled his makeshift sword, his 'secret thing', into the king's chamber.

Before we consider the horror that follows, it is worth considering this use of trickery. Ehud is not alone when it comes to such deception. In the preceding book, in Joshua 2, Rahab lied so the Israelite spies could make good their escape from Jericho. A few chapters later, the Gibeonites tricked Joshua into making a pact with them. Amazingly, God still blessed these people, not merely in spite of their trickery, but seemingly because of it!

So too with Ehud. Having tricked Eglon into a private meeting, he drew him deeper into his web, luring him to his feet with the words, 'I have a message *from God* for you' (v.20, emphasis added). He plunged his dagger into the king's belly, both losing the weapon in the folds of fat and causing, as the English Standard Version puts it, the 'dung' to come out.

With the king dead, Ehud demonstrated what a man of faith he was, as he boldly declared to the Israelites, 'the LORD has given Moab, your enemy, into your hands' (v.28). There is no doubt in Ehud's mind that Moab would fall. And God honours Ehud, granting him victory over the mighty army of Moab.

Though he used deceit and trickery, in the end, Ehud's faith is rewarded with the greatest legacy of all the judges: eighty years of peace.

Discussion Starters

1. What strikes you most in the story of Ehud's judgeship?

   _____

   _____

   _____

   _____

   _____

2. Ehud used trickery to fulfil God's task, and was blessed. Can you think of similar examples in the Bible? Do you believe these people acted in accordance with God's will?

   _____

   _____

   _____

   _____

   _____

3. Read 1 Samuel 16:1–4. God's call for deception has been compared with games like chess, where trickery and deceit play an important role in achieving victory. In what sort of circumstances might it be acceptable to use such tactics to carry out God's work today?

   _____

   _____

   _____

   _____

   _____

4. Like Shamgar with his oxgoad and Jael with her tent peg, Ehud used what he had to hand to do God's work. Can you think of other examples from the Bible of people using what they have (whether objects or abilities) for God?

_____
_____
_____
_____

5. Discuss your own areas of ability and gifting, and how these might be used in God's service.

_____
_____
_____
_____

6. Later in this book we will see the cry, 'For the LORD and for Gideon', but in verse 28 Ehud gives the glory only to God. 1 Corinthians 10:31 says, 'So whether you eat or drink or whatever you do, do it all for the glory of God.' How does this work out in practice?

_____
_____
_____
_____

7. Considering what we have learned about Ehud, why do you think God chose him to be Israel's judge?

_____
_____
_____
_____

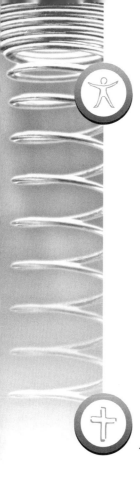

Personal Application

One of the great privileges of being a Christian is that God is constantly looking to use us for His glory. One of the great problems, however, is that we can so often feel inadequate or unworthy to work with Him. In Ehud we see a man who was willing to work with what he had – his cunning, his special dagger, his 'left-handedness' – and God used him to save Israel from the Moabites, bringing peace to the land for eighty years!

1 Peter 4:10 says, 'Each one should use whatever gift he has received to serve others, faithfully administering God's grace in its various forms.' Every day we have opportunities to use the things we have – our skills, our giftings, our abilities, our time and our possessions – to serve others and to serve God. What could be better than that?

Seeing Jesus in the Scriptures

Jesus came 'to serve, and to give his life as a ransom for many' (Mark 10:45). If there was ever someone used mightily by God, it was Him, and just look at the tools He used:

- Judas, who betrayed Jesus in Gethsemane;
- the Jewish priests, who rejected Him and called for His execution;
- Pontius Pilate, who authorised His death;
- the Roman soldiers, who flogged Him and crucified Him;
- the crude wooden cross to which He was nailed.

And as He hung there, Jesus took the punishment for our sin, so that we could be forgiven. Using what He had to hand, Jesus brought us peace with God – not just for eighty years, but for eternity.

WEEK 5

The Threefold Judge

Opening Icebreaker

It is against the law to drive in the UK without insurance, which is important for when accidents occur. It is also still a legal requirement for London taxis to carry oats and hay for horses, which is not quite so important. Go round the group thinking of other laws, and whether or not you believe it is important to obey them.

Bible Readings

- Judges 4:1–5:31 (if short of time just read Judges 4:1–9 and 15–22)
- Psalm 18:46–50
- Luke 22:42
- Philippians 2:6–8
- Hebrews 11:32–34

Key Verse: 'Barak said to her, "If you go with me, I will go; but if you don't go with me, I won't go."' (4:8)

Focus: God uses both discipline and blessing to grow our faith in Him.

Opening Our Eyes

Our third judge is really a trio of judges. We have
Deborah, a prophetess, who hears from God and
speaks on His behalf; Barak, a warrior, who defeats
the armies of the oppressor; and Jael, who slays the
oppressor. The account of their deeds is recorded in
both prose (chapter 4) and poetry (chapter 5).

As before, the Israelites did evil in the eyes of the Lord,
and this time He handed them over to the Canaanite king,
Jabin. He is a background figure, however, compared to
Sisera, the commander of his army. This Sisera, together
with his iron chariots, oppressed Israel for twenty years
until they cried out to the Lord.

Deborah, who was the leader of Israel thanks to her
prophetic gift, then called for Barak and gave him this
message: 'Go, take with you ten thousand men of Naphtali
and Zebulun and lead the way to Mount Tabor.
I (God) will lure Sisera ... with his chariots and his troops
to the Kishon River and give him into your hands' (vv.6–7).
Now, had Barak been a man of faith like Othniel or
Ehud, you would have expected immediate, unflinching
obedience. However, as the spiral of Judges continues its
downward trend, we see a less faith-filled response. He
would go, yes, but only on the condition that Deborah
accompanied him. As a result Deborah prophesied Barak
would lose the glory of killing Sisera – a woman would
kill him instead.

Clearly spurred by this painful proclamation, Barak
swiftly raised an army and headed, as commanded, to
Mount Tabor. In response, Sisera gathered his own army,
complete with chariots, and rushed out to punish the
Israelites for their impudence. Needless to say it didn't
quite work out that way!

As the troops prepared for battle, Deborah gave another message to Barak: 'Go! This is the day the LORD has given Sisera into your hands. Has not the LORD gone ahead of you?' (v.14). This time Barak had learned his lesson, and immediately led his army against the Canaanites and routed them. Seeing that he was defeated, Sisera escaped to his allies, the Kenites.

Here he ran into Jael, who must have seemed a real God-send. In a sense of course she was! Against all conventions Jael welcomed Sisera into her tent, covered him in a blanket, and gave him warm milk to calm him and ease him off to sleep. The deliberate, methodical assassination that followed is best seen in chapter 5:26–27: 'Her hand reached for the tent peg, her right hand for the workman's hammer. She struck Sisera, she crushed his head, she shattered and pierced his temple. At her feet he sank, he fell; there he lay. At her feet he sank, he fell; where he sank, there he fell – dead.' Note the hammer-like rhythm as Jael pinned him to the ground through his skull.

Though Barak lost the glory of killing Sisera, God was true to His word and gave him victory over the Canaanites. In response to this clear demonstration of God's sovereignty, Barak and Deborah burst into song – a song of faith, telling how God fought for Israel, sending the flood that immobilised the Canaanite chariots. So in the end, in glorious poetry, we see how Barak's faith was grown through God's discipline and blessing.

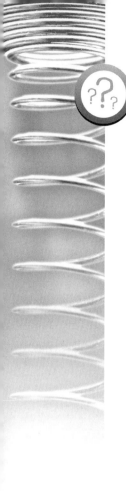

Discussion Starters

1. Of all the events that happen in these two chapters, what stands out the most for you?

   _____

   _____

   _____

   _____

   _____

2. Barak made it clear that his obedience to God's command was only on the condition that Deborah went with him (4:8). Why do you think he made this condition?

   _____

   _____

   _____

   _____

   _____

3. In response, God disciplined Barak by giving the glory of killing Sisera to Jael instead. However, He did not punish Barak, and the call to fight and the promise of victory remained. Discuss what you understand to be the difference between God's discipline and His punishment.

   _____

   _____

   _____

   _____

   _____

4. When the time for war arrived, the Lord ordered Barak to attack, and he obeyed without question. For this reason he is praised for his faith in Hebrews 11:32–34. What is the link between obedience and faith?

_____

_____

_____

_____

_____

5. During this account Barak's faith is grown, firstly through God's discipline in taking away the glory of killing Sisera, then through God's blessing in giving the Canaanites into his hand. Share examples from your own life where discipline or blessing from God has grown your faith in Him.

_____

_____

_____

_____

_____

6. The natural response of Deborah and Barak was to praise God. Read Psalm 18:46–50 to see a similar response from David when God saved him from Saul. What do you believe is the purpose of praise, and is it important?

_____

_____

_____

_____

_____

7. Take some time to share things in your own life for which you could praise God.

_____

_____

_____

_____

_____

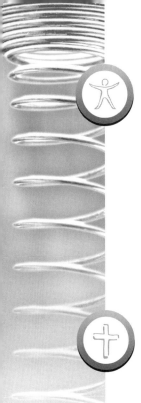

Personal Application

We tend to be very clear that Christianity is not about rules, but about having a relationship with God – a relationship that is built on grace and love, rather than obedience to laws. This is all true, but at the same time the Bible is full of commands for us to live in a certain way.

Among other things, we are called to love our enemies and our neighbours, to give ourselves to spreading the gospel, not chasing after money or possessions, and not worrying about the future. This is God showing us the best way to live. But do we really believe Him?

Seeing Jesus in the Scriptures

In Philippians 2, Paul also uses a poem to praise Jesus. Verses 6–8 are all about His unconditional obedience to the Father: '(He) being in very nature God, did not consider equality with God something to be grasped, but made himself nothing, taking the very nature of a servant, being made in human likeness. And being found in appearance as a man, he humbled himself and became obedient to death – even death on a cross!'

Jesus was sent with the hardest of all missions: subjected to a frail body like our own; rejected by His closest companions; beaten, whipped, spat on and humiliated; nailed to a cross to die in agony; and punished by God for our sin. And yet, even on the very evening He was betrayed, Jesus prayed, '… yet not my will, but yours be done' (Luke 22:42). Let's praise Him for His wonderful example of unconditional obedience!

WEEK 6

The Rise of Gideon

Opening Icebreaker

Think of some things in everyday life that you aren't sure you really trust. For example:
- Sports massage – I know it's supposed to do me good, but it feels like it's actually damaging me.
- Online banking – I am assured it is all secure, but how can I be sure that someone won't hack in and spend lots of money (that I don't have)?

Bible Readings

- Judges 6:1–7:25 (if short of time just read Judges 6:16–27 and 6:36–7:8)
- Matthew 4:5–7
- Hebrews 12:10–11
- James 1:2–4

Key Verse: 'When Gideon heard the dream and its interpretation, he worshipped God. He returned to the camp of Israel and called out, "Get up! The LORD has given the Midianite camp into your hands."' (7:15)

Focus: God is committed to growing our faith.

Opening Our Eyes

Though Gideon is famous for his lack of faith, in
Hebrews 11 he is among those commended for their
faith. The first half of his story shows us how this change
came about. Israel's oppressor at this time was Midian,
whose men and camels are compared with 'swarms of
locusts … impossible to count' (Judg. 6:5). This vast hoard
ransacked the land, destroying the crops and taking the
livestock. The few crops the Israelites managed to save
had to be hidden away to avoid being stolen.

For this reason, we meet our hero-to-be threshing wheat,
not in the open, but hidden from view in a winepress.
It was here that an angel brought him the message: 'Go
in the strength you have and save Israel out of Midian's
hand. Am I not sending you?' (v.14). Gideon, it seems,
was not convinced that God *was* sending him, and so
there follows a series of tests, with Gideon testing God,
and God in return testing Gideon. The first was Gideon's
request, in verse 17, for a sign that this was really a
message from God. He then hurried off to get some meat
and bread for the angel, and on his return the angel
touched the food with his staff, causing it to be consumed
by fire. Gideon got his sign!

In return God tested Gideon with the command: '"Tear
down your father's altar to Baal and cut down the
Asherah pole beside it"' (v.25). This may not seem like
a big deal, but this would be comparable to God calling
you to set fire to a mosque or tear up all the anti-Christian
books in your local library. Smashing up his town's centre
of worship was no small thing – no wonder he did it by
night! But he did do it, and he nearly ended up being
dragged off by the lynch mob.

Spurred on by his success, and empowered by the Spirit
of the Lord, Gideon rounded up a substantial army to

take on the Midianites – 32,000 men in all. However, Gideon still lacked the faith to go to war, and so he asked God to prove Israel would win by wetting a fleece, but not the ground. After this came to pass, he asked God to confirm that this really was definitely His doing, and not mere coincidence, by wetting the ground but not the fleece. God graciously did as requested, but in return for these two tests, He also tested Gideon twice.

There's a wonderful statement from God in Judges 7:2: 'You have too many men for me to deliver Midian into their hands.' It sounds crazy, but God wanted there to be no doubt that it was He who had saved them. So He ordered Gideon to let those who were scared go home. A massive 22,000 of them departed, but even then God was not satisfied. 'There are still too many men. Take them down to the water, and I will sift them for you there.' (v.4) This sifting was based on the seemingly arbitrary test of how they drank water, whether directly from the source or via their hands. The result was that a mere three hundred, less than one per cent of the original army, remained to fight against the Midianites.

Finally, Gideon was ready for battle and, full of faith, he called his men to action. 'Get up! The LORD has given the Midianite camp into your hands.' (v.15)

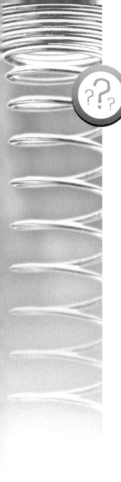

Discussion Starters

1. What do you find most striking about this first part of Gideon's judgeship?

_____

_____

_____

_____

_____

2. Gideon tested God three times. Why do you think he did this?

_____

_____

_____

_____

_____

3. Read Matthew 4:5–7. Here Jesus quotes Deuteronomy 6:16: 'Do not put the LORD your God to the test'. What, if any, is the difference between Satan's attempt to get Jesus to test God, and Gideon's three tests of God?

_____

_____

_____

_____

_____

4. In return God tested Gideon three times. What was His aim in doing this?

_____

_____

_____

_____

_____

5. Read Hebrews 12:10–11. How do these verses relate to the testing of Gideon? And how do they relate to us as God's children?

_____

_____

_____

_____

_____

6. Faith, as we have seen, is of great importance for us as God's people. How might we learn from Gideon's example as we seek to grow in our faith?

_____

_____

_____

_____

_____

7. Share experiences of testing from God in your own life that has built your faith. Are there specific areas where you want to grow in faith?

_____

_____

_____

_____

_____

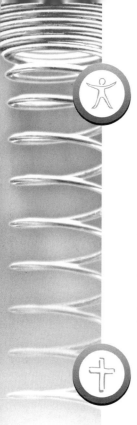

Personal Application

Our faith shows the depth of our relationship with God – the more we love Him, the more we will trust and believe Him. Because of this, God is committed to building our faith, and will take us through times of testing, not to destroy our faith, but to develop it. James opened his letter with the challenge: 'Consider it pure joy, my brothers, whenever you face trials of many kinds, because you know that the testing of your faith develops perseverance. Perseverance must finish its work so that you may be mature and complete, not lacking anything' (James 1:2–4). While these tests may be far from what we think of as 'pure joy', they are for our good. Do we believe our faith is worth such testing?

Seeing Jesus in the Scriptures

'Your faith has healed you.' 'Woman, you have great faith!' 'I have prayed ... that your faith may not fail.' 'Have faith in God.' Jesus was constantly looking for faith in the people He met – rebuking His disciples when they lacked it, teaching about the importance of it and often commenting when He saw it in others. In His own home town of Capernaum, the people's lack of faith resulted in a lack of healing. Jesus wanted to work together with those who had faith, who trusted and believed in Him.

And as Jesus hung on the cross, He demonstrated the greatest faith in God when, trusting His sacrifice was sufficient and believing He would rise again, He said, 'Father, into your hands I commit my spirit' (Luke 23:46).

WEEK 7

The Fall of Gideon

Opening Icebreaker

There are all kinds of things that can take up our time and our energy. Go round the group thinking of some examples, such as television, stamp-collecting or DIY.

Bible Readings

- Judges 8:1–35 (if short on time just read verses 1–9, 13–17 and 22–27)
- 1 Samuel 23:9–12
- 1 Corinthians 10:11–12
- 1 John 5:21

Key Verse: 'Gideon made the gold into an ephod, which he placed in Ophrah, his town. All Israel prostituted themselves by worshipping it there, and it became a snare to Gideon and his family.' (8:27)

Focus: Beware of idols! They can seriously damage your faith in God.

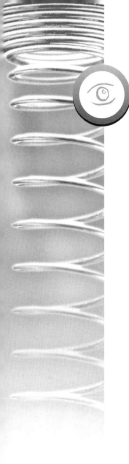

Opening Our Eyes

In our previous session we saw Gideon grow in his faith
in God to the point that, with a mere 300 men, he took
on the vast army of the Midianites. 'For the LORD and for
Gideon,' his men cried as they pursued their scattered
enemy across the country. Sadly in this last chapter of his
judgeship, it appears it was more for Gideon than for the
Lord.

Gideon starts out well in chapter 8, exercising great
diplomacy with the argumentative Ephraimites. But as
he crossed the Jordan, hot on the heels of the Midianite
kings, he seems to have become a different man – no
longer the diplomat, but the despot! At the town of
Succoth his request for bread to feed his men was turned
down by the officials, so Gideon promised, 'I will tear
your flesh with desert thorns and briars' (v.7). Suffering
the same refusal at Peniel, Gideon vowed to return to tear
down their tower.

Eventually Gideon captured the Midianite kings, Zebah
and Zalmunna, and took them into custody. He then
returned to wreak the promised vengeance upon those
two towns, first pulling down the tower at Peniel and
killing all the men, then gathering the leaders of Succoth
and thrashing them with thorny branches. Finally, after
years of struggling against foreign enemies, Israel's
downward spiral had brought them to the point of turning
on each other.

Assured of victory, the Israelites called on Gideon to
be their king: 'Rule over us – you, your son and your
grandson ...' (v.22). Gideon's response looks at first to
be one of great spiritual maturity: 'I will not rule over
you, nor will my son rule over you. The LORD will rule
over you' (v.23). But let us consider the evidence:

- Having slain the Midianite kings (v.21), Gideon took for *himself* the kingly ornaments that hung on their camels' necks.
- After refusing the kingship, he immediately requested gold earrings from the plunder – almost twenty kilos in all (vv.24–25).
- Verses 30 and 31 tell us Gideon had many wives and even a concubine.
- There is the assumption in chapter 9 that his seventy sons would rule after his death.
- And, even more telling, the son of Gideon's concubine was called Abimelech, meaning 'my father the king'.

These speak clearly of Gideon's role as king, at least in practice if not in name. Though it was God who really saved the Israelites, Gideon appears to have been seduced by the power of leading them to victory.

But Gideon's real fall came when he took all those gold earrings and fashioned them into an ephod – a special, priestly device used for discerning God's will (see 1 Samuel 23:9–12 for an example of this being practised). No one is entirely sure how an ephod worked, but clearly Gideon wanted to have a quick, easy way to know what God's will was in any given situation. Since Gideon had not spoken with God since he went up against the Midianites, an ephod would just have to do instead. But far from building the faith of Gideon and the Israelites, 'All Israel prostituted themselves by worshipping it (the ephod) there, and it became a snare to Gideon and his family' (v.27). It is a sad conclusion to the account of this former man of faith and, in the end, it was Gideon himself who drew the Israelites away from serving God.

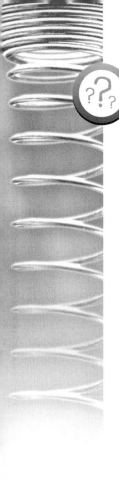

Discussion Starters

1. What struck you most in this final chapter of Gideon's judgeship?

    _____

    _____

    _____

    _____

    _____

2. Gideon suddenly seems to change for the worse from verse 4 onwards. What do you suspect was the reason for this?

    _____

    _____

    _____

    _____

    _____

3. There is no evidence of conversation between God and Gideon after the battle (see Judg. 7:9). How do you think this affected Gideon's decisions? Have you experienced times when God seemed silent?

    _____

    _____

    _____

    _____

    _____

4. Having defeated the Midianites and their kings, it appears Gideon forgot he owed all this to God, and so began to behave as if he was the king (despite turning the role down). Consider whether there have been situations where you have forgotten to give the credit to God when He has worked in your life.

_____

_____

_____

_____

_____

5. Why do you think the ephod had such a negative
effect on Gideon and the Israelites? Would a device
for discerning God's will be detrimental to our walk
with God today?

_____

_____

_____

_____

_____

6. The idols in the ancient world were mostly handmade
objects, which seem alien to our modern 'enlightened'
thinking. If an idol is anything that draws us away
from God, or seeks to take God's place in our lives,
what might be considered idols today?

_____

_____

_____

_____

_____

7. Share examples of some of the idols that you have
struggled with, and discuss how it is possible to guard
yourselves against them.

_____

_____

_____

_____

_____

Personal Application

On this first leg of our journey through Judges, there has been much to inspire us and to help us grow in faith. However, this last session confronts us with the danger of being drawn away from God. Gideon had become a man of great faith, but he was seduced by power and ensnared by his ephod.

In 1 Corinthians 10, speaking about Israel's past, Paul wrote: 'These things happened to them as examples and were written down as warnings for us ... So, if you think you are standing firm, be careful that you don't fall!' (vv.11–12). No matter how great our faith or how firmly we stand in God, no one is immune to idolatry!

John's first epistle closes with the warning: 'Dear children, keep yourselves from idols' (1 John 5:21). Idols can come in any shape or form to destroy our faith in God. Are we ready to war against them?

Seeing Jesus in the Scriptures

Throughout His life, Jesus suffered constant attack to undermine His faith in God:
• Satan tempted Him in the wilderness.
• A great crowd attempted to make Him their king.
• His own disciples tried to dissuade Him from going to Jerusalem to complete His mission.

Yet unlike Gideon, Jesus never took His eyes off the Father, and at no point did He waver in His faith. Because He made sure that God was at the centre of His life, there was no idol in the world that could seduce Jesus and keep Him from completing His mission to save the world.

Leader's Notes

These notes are designed to help you lead these sessions in a group. Please do read through the notes before each session to help with your preparation. It is also worth reading through the 'Personal Application' and 'Seeing Jesus in the Scriptures' sections to get a feel for the direction of the session in question.

The overarching theme of these first eight chapters of the book of Judges is faith – the importance of faith, the effects of faith, ways in which it is grown and developed, and ways in which it can be undermined and even destroyed.

Week 1: Land Not Taken

This first session introduces us to the topic of faith, and reveals the way our actions are shaped by our faith (or lack of it). Having faith in God's promises to us is also an important part of this session.

Opening Icebreaker:

The aim is to get the group to see the connection between what we believe and what we do, and between faith and trust.

Bible Readings:

All the sessions in this book have a number of verses from other parts of the Bible. It is not necessary to read these together at the beginning, as they are mainly used in the Discussion Starters, but it would be beneficial to read the main passage together. As this session covers more than a chapter of Judges, it may be best to read through the key sections as listed, and ask the group to read the whole passage before you meet together.

Key Verse:

This verse shows the core problem with the faith of the Israelites, which led to them not only failing to drive out the inhabitants, but also to the stern judgment delivered by the angel of the Lord. Despite the promise that God was with them, when the Israelites came face to face with their enemies, their faith in God proved not to be strong enough.

Discussion Starters:

1. Although the excuses in verses 27 and 34 are almost amusingly poor, there may be mixed opinions on how reasonable these excuses were. It is worth bearing in mind that, back in Judges 2:1, God had *promised* to give them the land. Also have a look at Joshua's response to the iron chariots in Joshua 17:18.

2. Deuteronomy 7:2 says, '... and when the LORD your God has delivered them over to you and you have defeated them, then you must destroy them totally. Make no treaty with them, and show them no mercy.'

In the two asides listed in this Discussion Starter, the Israelites failed to do what God had commanded. Firstly they only mutilated Adoni-Bezek, rather than killing him (though Adoni-Bezek is said to have been killed in Jerusalem, it is unclear exactly when this happened). In the second, they made a treaty with a man from Luz, sparing his life, only to have him build a replacement, non-Israelite city.

3. Give an example first to get the ball rolling. For example, 'I believe that the Bible will help to guide me through life (Psa. 119:105), therefore I read and meditate on it.' Or 'In Genesis 6, God commanded Noah to build the ark to save himself and his family from the coming judgment. Noah clearly believed God, because he then built the ark.'

4. The 'trust' aspect of faith is important in answering this question. Christianity is primarily about entering into a loving relationship with God as our Father. Trust is a fundamental part of such a relationship, and therefore faith is of great importance to God. To help get across the connection between faith and trust, it is worth mentioning some of the examples that were considered in the icebreaker.

5. The excuses that were considered in the opening discussion starter will help here. It can be easy to start criticising the Israelites at this point in the discussion. Instead, encourage the group to imagine how they themselves might have acted in such a hostile situation.

6. There are only four promises listed here (I say 'only', but they are four fantastic ones!). Feel free to ask people what their own favourite biblical promises are, and how these shape the way they live.

7. It is worth bearing in mind that God's promise to give them the land was not cancelled, rather it was delayed due to the Israelites' lack of faith. That generation certainly never received it, and it was not until the reigns of David and Solomon that the land was finally taken, and it was lost again soon enough! Some people in the group may have personal promises given to them from God, and if they are willing to discuss them it would be good to apply this question to such promises as well.

Week 2: The Shape of Things to Come

This session looks at the cycle that will be repeated throughout Judges, focussing particularly on the root issue of the Israelites failing to teach the next generation about the Lord. God's discipline of His children is also considered.

Opening Icebreaker:

The aim is to get the group to think about those who have taught them about the Lord, focussing on the people who helped them to understand the gospel.

Bible Readings:

Again this is a fairly long passage. The suggested verses of chapter 2 detail the cycle and its cause, so just reading this would suffice. As before, the other readings will mostly be dealt with in the Discussion Starters.

Key Verse:

This is the verse which reveals the root cause for the Israelites' constant failure to remain faithful to God. Note that not only did they not know the Lord, but they did not even know about the things He had done for Israel.

Discussion Starters:

1. This first Discussion Starter is closely linked with the second, and you may find that while discussing the cycle from the Israelites' point of view, the groups will naturally start considering God's purpose as well. This is fine, and you may want to draw the group's attention to the second Discussion Starter at this point, but it is worth sticking with the human point of view for a while.

2. When considering God's purpose, tackle the perceived difference between punishment and discipline. Some may see this cycle, which includes some horrific treatment of Israel by her enemies, as cruel and vindictive, while others may see this as God's only option if He wants to train His people and bring them back to faith. It is worth bearing in mind what Hebrews 12 has to say about God's discipline.

3. Building on the second Discussion Starter, this turns the focus on Christians today. This could open up quite a lengthy and difficult discussion, as it is hard to remain objective about personal suffering and the suffering of those we know and love. Do encourage the group to share examples whether from their own lives or the lives of others.

4. These three passages lay the responsibility for teaching the next generation firmly at the feet of the Levitical priesthood and the parents, so these two groups are the focus of this discussion starter. The discussion will naturally be fairly speculative, as we cannot really know why they failed in this vital duty, but the aim here is to get the group to think about why God's people might choose not to pass on the truth about God, in preparation for the next two Discussion Starters.

5. On the face of it, this is looking for a quick answer rather than a discussion. However, it is worth taking the time to ensure everyone understands the opening statement about the 'next generation', and whether the group agrees with this definition. Also, if you take the time to read the great commission in Matthew 28, draw attention to the word 'teaching' in verse 20.

6. The aim of this Discussion Starter is not only to get the group to think in general terms about why Christians might fail to pass on the truth about God, but also to

give them the opportunity to consider anything that might keep, and maybe *has* kept, them from passing it on themselves.

It may be worth reminding the group of the icebreaker, where they were reminded that, in order to come to faith themselves, someone had to tell them the truth about God.

7. As mentioned in the Discussion Starter, we will focus more on idols in session 7. The aim here is not only to consider objective ways prosperity can affect our faith, but for the group to think about their own personal walk with God. If you have personally struggled with prosperity in your walk with God, it would be good to give this as an example to help others to open up. This would be a good opportunity to pray with one another if there are those who struggle with this particular idol.

Week 3: Othniel: The Foremost Judge

This is our first session that deals with a judge, and the focus is on working together with God to accomplish His will, together with what it means to be filled with and led by the Holy Spirit.

Opening Icebreaker:

There will hopefully be a wide range of opinions about team games versus singles games, and the aim is to get the group to think about working together with others.

Bible Readings:

The account of Othniel is very short, and it may be a good opportunity to read it in a few different translations, depending on the versions available in the group. (Cushan-Rishathaim is pronounced as written, with a long 'a' and a long 'i' at the end.)

Key Verse:

The reason for choosing this verse will become apparent
as you read the 'Opening Our Eyes' section. In brief, the
phrase 'who saved them' is a single word in Hebrew,
yoshiem, and either the LORD or Othniel could be the
subject. The implication is that they worked together in
unison to carry out the salvation of Israel.

Discussion Starters:

1. This open question for people to share what was most
striking for them from the passage will be the starter
for each of the remaining sessions. The aim here is to
encourage discussion, and so avoid getting bogged down
with details.

2. It may be helpful to briefly recap on the main points
of the previous session, with a focus on the purpose of
discipline.

3. This has the potential to be a fairly lengthy time of
sharing, but it is worth taking the time, as remembering
what God has done in our lives is a great way to build
our faith. To get the ball rolling it would be good to start
sharing an example from your own life.

4. To help with this question, read the earlier account of
Othniel in Judges 1:11–15. The narrator has included this
for a reason, as background to Othniel's judgeship. As
such we see a man who has already been faithful and
courageous, whom God then chose to save His people.

5. Looking at other passages where the Spirit of the Lord
comes upon people will aid discussion. For example:
Judges 6:34ff; 14:5–6; 1 Samuel 10:6; 2 Chronicles 24:20;
Luke 4:1ff. The key point to bring out is that the Holy
Spirit empowers people to carry out God's will.

6. Having considered the great deeds of the Spirit-filled heroes of Scripture, this question turns the spotlight on the everyday life of the Spirit-filled believer today. The daily, moment-by-moment guidance of the Holy Spirit, combined with our choice to work together with Him and follow His leading, is the focus here. It may be worth bringing in some of the pros of team games that were raised in the icebreaker to help the discussion.

7. This would be a good opportunity to pray for one another, and to discuss the practicalities of our daily walk with God.

Week 4: Ehud: A Man with a Message

WARNING! In this session a man is killed in a highly graphic and unpleasant manner. Our focus as we consider the account of Ehud is on the fact that God uses people of faith just as they are, wherever they are. The use of cunning and trickery to do God's work is also considered.

Opening Icebreaker:

The aim of this icebreaker is to start to think about how various objects can be used in a variety of different and unexpected ways (with the eventual link that God can use us in any circumstance).

Bible Readings:

This fairly brief passage from Judges 3 is dealt with excellently in the English Standard Version if you have a copy to hand.

Key Verse:

The word 'message' also means 'thing', and this verse highlights Ehud's cunning and deceit which he employed in saving Israel.

Discussion Starters:

1. No doubt the gory account of Eglon's death will be at the forefront of people's minds here, but it is worth holding out to see what else struck people in this story.

2. Some other examples of using trickery to fulfil God's will are Jacob tricking Isaac into blessing him (Gen. 27), Joseph concealing his identity from his brothers in order to test them (Gen. 42–44), David tricking Achish into thinking he was mad (1 Sam. 21).

3. The question implies that trickery and deceit are an acceptable way to carry out God's work, and no doubt opinions on this will be mixed. Some modern-day examples of such things which might be considered acceptable include the smuggling of Bibles into China, the hiding of Jews from the Nazis in World War 2, and churches running outreach events that sneak in a gospel message.

4. The key here is that God can use us with whatever skills, gifts and resources we have to hand. In addition to the examples of Shamgar, Jael and Samson, the book of Judges has an account of a woman who wounded Abimelech with a millstone, and of Gideon who used horns, jars and torches to rout the Midianites.

5. Most people will be reluctant to put forward their own areas of ability and gifting, and this is really an opportunity for the group to suggest what they see as being each other's abilities and areas of gifting. This can

be a very encouraging exercise, especially in light of the fact that God uses people where they are with what they have to hand.

6. This question really has two angles to it. The first is to look at the things we do and ask ourselves whether they glorify God. The second is to consider how to give glory to God in the midst of all that we do – especially the things we might consider mundane or unspiritual.

7. There may be mixed feelings about Ehud, considering his deceit and his horrific assassination of Eglon. Remind the group of Ehud's faith in God, and his desire that the glory should go to Him. It just goes to show that God can use anyone who has faith in Him!

Week 5: The Threefold Judge

WARNING! There is an even more brutal murder in this session. In this, and the following session, the focus is on God's commitment to growing our faith, and the ways in which He does this.

Opening Icebreaker:

The aim here is for the group to think how easy it is to be selective in our obedience. This is a great opportunity for people to come out with all those ridiculous laws they have come across. It is worth throwing in speed limits which, though important, almost all drivers present will have disobeyed!

Bible Readings:

This session covers two chapters, the second being a poetic retelling of the first. The two shorter passages suggested give the main points for discussion, though again it is worth getting the group to read through at least the whole of chapter 4 beforehand.

Key Verse:

This verse shows Barak's conditional obedience to God's command, which cost him the glory of killing the oppressor of Israel.

Discussion Starters:

1. As with Ehud, the gruesome nature of the murder needs to be dealt with first, so other striking points can be considered.

2. It is likely this will come up in discussing the previous point. There will be those who see Barak's faith in wanting Deborah to accompany him to inform him of God's will, and those who see Barak as lacking in faith. Either way, his response is clear – had Deborah not gone with him, he would have disobeyed God's command.

3. This will be considered further in the next study, but look at Hebrews 12:5–11 to get across the idea that 'discipline' is done out of love. Also worth bearing in mind is the fact that Jesus took on Himself all our punishment, leaving none for us!

4. The link between faith and obedience was touched on in session 1, and you may also want to link in the selective obedience of the icebreaker.

5. Have an example ready to share with the group to encourage others to share. Examples can be either of God exercising discipline, and so growing faith, or of God blessing, through such things as answered prayer or proving Himself faithful to His promises, and so growing faith.

6. This is a quick question to prepare the group for the next Discussion Starter. Key points for praise are acknowledgement, giving thanks and giving glory to God for the things He has done.

7. In addition to sharing items of possible praise, this would be a good opportunity to spend some time in prayer, actively praising God for these things He has done.

Week 6: The Rise of Gideon

Following on from the previous session, the focus here is on God's commitment to growing our faith, and further ways this is accomplished.

Opening Icebreaker:

The aim of this icebreaker is to consider ways we can lack faith in everyday things.

Bible Readings:

The account of Gideon is the second longest after Samson. As such it is more important than ever that the group read through chapters six and seven beforehand, though the two passages suggested contain most of what will be discussed later.

Key Verse:

Although this verse is outside those suggested, it shows the moment when Gideon's faith had grown to the point that he was ready to trust God to give the Midianites into his hands.

Discussion Starters:

1. As there is a lot that could be striking in this account, try not to spend too long on this point.

2. It is worth reminding the group that the Midianite army was immense, as it can be easy to condemn Gideon for his lack of faith.

3. Deuteronomy 6:16 refers to the episode at Massah in Exodus 17. At this time the Israelites tested God, not because they wanted to have more faith in Him, but because they wanted to prove Him wrong. Similarly, Satan was trying to get Jesus to doubt God. By contrast, Gideon seems to have tested God, because he wanted to have faith. Remember then, far from rebuking Gideon, God honoured Gideon's requests.

4. Bearing in mind what we have seen in previous sessions, that faith is demonstrated through obedience, God immediately tested Gideon's faith by giving Him outrageous commands. It is worth considering how this would have, in turn, increased his faith.

5. These verses talk about the 'harvest of righteousness and peace' that God's discipline produces in us. First discuss how these relate to faith (righteousness and peace both being products of our faith in God), before considering how this relates both to Gideon and to ourselves. It may be worth reminding the group of Barak's faith being grown through discipline in the previous session.

6. The focus here is not only on God testing us, but also on us testing God. In the light of Discussion Starter 3, it is worth discussing whether it would be appropriate for us to 'lay out fleeces' before God.

7. It is best to keep this discussion in two distinct parts: firstly sharing experience of God growing our faith; and secondly sharing areas where people want to grow in faith. This would be a good opportunity to pray into some of these areas, especially asking for opportunities to grow in faith.

Week 7: The Fall of Gideon

In this final session, having spent so long thinking about the growth of our faith in God, we are faced with the idea of our faith being damaged and even destroyed. Our main focus will be on idolatry, and it is important to be clear that idolatry today has little to do with worshipping bits of carved wood and stone, and much more to do with the draw of worldliness, such as the love of money, power, possessions, achievement and so on. All such things have the potential to draw us away from God and cause our faith in Him to dwindle.

Opening Icebreaker:

To help the group begin to think about the reality of idolatry today, this icebreaker aims to get each person to identify some of those things that take up our time and our energy (and therefore, ultimately, our worship).

Bible Readings:

This chapter may well be short enough to read as a group, but the three sections suggested will bring out the main points that will be discussed later if there is insufficient time. As before, it is worth asking the group to read the whole chapter before you meet together.

Key Verse:

In this verse we see the ephod – an ostensibly holy object that was intended to be used by the priests to discern God's will – which became an idol not only to Gideon, but to the whole nation of Israel.

Discussion Starters:

2. It is, of course, impossible to be sure what changed Gideon's attitude. One plausible suggestion is that Gideon was forced to be diplomatic with the Ephraimites, as this was a whole tribe (numbered at 32,500 in Numbers 26:37), who seem to always be itching for a fight. Succoth and Peniel, on the other hand, were small cities with maybe fewer fighting men than Gideon had, so he could afford to be harsh with them.

3. Before the battle with the Midianites, the Lord spoke to Gideon eleven times. The silence that follows is therefore quite a stark contrast, and it is easy to imagine Gideon feeling somewhat rudderless as a result. Sharing experiences of God seeming silent may well lead to a discussion about how to hear God, which you might consider worth giving some time to.

4. There could be disagreement over whether Gideon really behaved like a king, so repeat the points listed in the 'Opening Our Eyes' section. The main aim of this Discussion Starter is to get the group to think about ways God has been working in their own lives. As usual when it comes to sharing, it is worth having an example to start the ball rolling.

5. 'Relationship' is a key word to use here. As humans, we tend to prefer a list of rules for what to do and what not to do rather than having to keep asking God. The problem is that the moment we come up with such a list,

our communication with God tends to all but disappear. An ephod would have much the same effect. A good verse to use is Romans 7:6, which says, '... we have been released from the law so that we serve in the new way of the Spirit, and not in the old way of the written code.' This goes back to keeping in step with the Spirit, which we looked at in session 3 – it is about being attentive to the guidance of the Holy Spirit, working together in partnership with Him.

6. The various things that were mentioned in the icebreaker can be added to the list here and may help the group to identify a number of other such potential idols. Bear in mind that it is perfectly legitimate for Christians to have hobbies and possessions. The aim here is not to condemn such practices, but to raise awareness that even the most innocuous of such things can become an idol.

7. Again, a personal example would be useful to get the discussion going. There will no doubt be a number of suggestions as to how to guard against idols, including getting rid of the items in question, and devising ways of thinking about other things, but such tactics only solve half of the problem. If you remove an idol there are plenty more ready to take its place. The key is to ensure that God is the centre of your life – when He is in His rightful place as the most important person in your life, and the focus of your faith, there will be no room left for idols.

National Distributors

UK: (and countries not listed below)

CWR, Waverley Abbey House, Waverley Lane, Farnham, Surrey GU9 8EP.
Tel: (01252) 784700 Outside UK (44) 1252 784700 Email: mail@cwr.org.uk

AUSTRALIA: KI Entertainment, Unit 21 317-321 Woodpark Road, Smithfield, New South Wales 2164.
Tel: 1 800 850 777 Fax: 02 9604 3699 Email: sales@kientertainment.com.au

CANADA: David C Cook Distribution Canada, PO Box 98, 55 Woodslee Avenue, Paris, Ontario N3L 3E5.
Tel: 1800 263 2664 Email: sandi.swanson@davidccook.ca

GHANA: Challenge Enterprises of Ghana, PO Box 5723, Accra.
Tel: (021) 222437/223249 Fax: (021) 226227 Email: ceg@africaonline.com.gh

HONG KONG: Cross Communications Ltd, 1/F, 562A Nathan Road, Kowloon.
Tel: 2780 1188 Fax: 2770 6229 Email: cross@crosshk.com

INDIA: Crystal Communications, 10-3-18/4/1, East Marredpalli, Secunderabad – 500026,
Andhra Pradesh. Tel/Fax: (040) 27737145 Email: crystal_edwj@rediffmail.com

KENYA: Keswick Books and Gifts Ltd, PO Box 10242-00400, Nairobi.
Tel: (020) 2226047/312639 Email: sales.keswick@africaonline.co.ke

MALAYSIA: Canaanland, No. 25 Jalan PJU 1A/41B, NZX Commercial Centre, Ara Jaya, 47301
Petaling Jaya, Selangor. Tel: (03) 7885 0540/1/2 Fax: (03) 7885 0545 Email: info@canaanland.com.my

Salvation Publishing & Distribution Sdn Bhd, 23 Jalan SS 2/64, 47300 Petaling Jaya, Selangor.
Tel: (03) 78766411/78766797 Fax: (03) 78757066/78756360 Email: info@salvationbookcentre.com

NEW ZEALAND: KI Entertainment, Unit 21 317-321 Woodpark Road, Smithfield, New South Wales
2164, Australia. Tel: 0 800 850 777 Fax: +612 9604 3699 Email: sales@kientertainment.com.au

NIGERIA: FBFM, Helen Baugh House, 96 St Finbarr's College Road, Akoka, Lagos.
Tel: (01) 7747429/4700218/825775/827264 Email: fbfm_1@yahoo.com

PHILIPPINES: OMF Literature Inc, 776 Boni Avenue, Mandaluyong City.
Tel: (02) 531 2183 Fax: (02) 531 1960 Email: gloadlaon@omflit.com

SINGAPORE: Alby Commercial Enterprises Pte Ltd, 95 Kallang Avenue #04-00, AIS Industrial
Building, 339420. Tel: (65) 629 27238 Fax: (65) 629 27235 Email: marketing@alby.com.sg

SOUTH AFRICA: Struik Christian Books, 80 MacKenzie Street, PO Box 1144, Cape Town 8000.
Tel: (021) 462 4360 Fax: (021) 461 3612 Email: info@struikchristianmedia.co.za

SRI LANKA: Christombu Publications (Pvt) Ltd, Bartleet House, 65 Braybrooke Place, Colombo 2.
Tel: (9411) 2421073/2447665 Email: dhanad@bartleet.com

USA: David C Cook Distribution Canada, PO Box 98, 55 Woodslee Avenue, Paris, Ontario N3L 3E5,
Canada. Tel: 1800 263 2664 Email: sandi.swanson@davidccook.ca

Courses and seminars

Publishing and new media

Conference facilities

Transforming lives

CWR's vision is to enable people to experience personal transformation through applying God's Word to their lives and relationships.

Our Bible-based training and resources help people around the world to:
• Grow in their walk with God
• Understand and apply Scripture to their lives
• Resource themselves and their church
• Develop pastoral care and counselling skills
• Train for leadership
• Strengthen relationships, marriage and family life
and much more.

Our insightful writers provide daily Bible-reading notes and other resources for all ages, and our experienced course designers and presenters have gained an international reputation for excellence and effectiveness.

CWR's Training and Conference Centre in Surrey, England, provides excellent facilities in an idyllic setting – ideal for both learning and spiritual refreshment.

CWR Applying God's Word
to everyday life and relationships

CWR, Waverley Abbey House,
Waverley Lane, Farnham,
Surrey GU9 8EP, UK

Telephone: **+44 (0)1252 784700**
Email: info@cwr.org.uk
Website: www.cwr.org.uk

Registered Charity No 294387
Company Registration No 1990308

Dramatic new resource

Names of God - Exploring the depths of God's character
by Mary Evans

Examine the names of God in the Old Testament and the titles ascribed in the New Testament to Jesus and the Holy Spirit, and discover some startling truths about *who* God is.

72-page booklet, 148x210mm
ISBN: 978-1-85345-680-0

The bestselling *Cover to Cover* Bible Study Series

1 Corinthians
Growing a Spirit-filled church
ISBN: 978-1-85345-374-8

2 Corinthians
Restoring harmony
ISBN: 978-1-85345-551-3

1 Timothy
Healthy churches –
effective Christians
ISBN: 978-1-85345-291-8

23rd Psalm
The Lord is my shepherd
ISBN: 978-1-85345-449-3

2 Timothy and Titus
Vital Christianity
ISBN: 978-1-85345-338-0

Acts 1-12
Church on the move
ISBN: 978-1-85345-574-2

Acts 13-28
To the ends of the earth
ISBN: 978-1-85345-592-6

Ecclesiastes
Hard questions and
spiritual answers
ISBN: 978-1-85345-371-7

Elijah
A man and his God
ISBN: 978-1-85345-575-9

Ephesians
Claiming your inheritance
ISBN: 978-1-85345-229-1

Esther
For such a time as this
ISBN: 978-1-85345-511-7

Fruit of the Spirit
Growing more like Jesus
ISBN: 978-1-85345-375-5

Galatians
Freedom in Christ
ISBN: 978-1-85345-648-0

Genesis 1-11
Foundations of reality
ISBN: 978-1-85345-404-2

God's Rescue Plan
Finding God's fingerprints
on human history
ISBN: 978-1-85345-294-9

Great Prayers of the Bible
Applying them to our lives today
ISBN: 978-1-85345-253-6

Hebrews
Jesus – simply the best
ISBN: 978-1-85345-337-3

Hosea
The love that never fails
ISBN: 978-1-85345-290-1

Isaiah 1-39
Prophet to the nations
ISBN: 978-1-85345-510-0

Isaiah 40-66
Prophet of restoration
ISBN: 978-1-85345-550-6

James
Faith in action
ISBN: 978-1-85345-293-2

Jeremiah
The passionate prophet
ISBN: 978-1-85345-372-4

John's Gospel
Exploring the seven miraculous signs
ISBN: 978-1-85345-295-6

Joseph
The power of forgiveness and reconciliation
ISBN: 978-1-85345-252-9

Judges 1–8
The spiral of faith
ISBN: 978-1-85345-681-7

Mark
Life as it is meant to be lived
ISBN: 978-1-85345-233-8

Moses
Face to face with God
ISBN: 978-1-85345-336-6

Names of God
Exploring the depths of God's character
ISBN: 978-1-85345-680-0

Nehemiah
Principles for life
ISBN: 978-1-85345-335-9

Parables
Communicating God on earth
ISBN: 978-1-85345-340-3

Philemon
From slavery to freedom
ISBN: 978-1-85345-453-0

Philippians
Living for the sake of the gospel
ISBN: 978-1-85345-421-9

Prayers of Jesus
Hearing His heartbeat
ISBN: 978-1-85345-647-3

Proverbs
Living a life of wisdom
ISBN: 978-1-85345-373-1

Revelation 1–3
Christ's call to the Church
ISBN: 978-1-85345-461-5

Revelation 4–22
The Lamb wins! Christ's final victory
ISBN: 978-1-85345-411-0

Rivers of Justice
Responding to God's call to righteousness today
ISBN: 978-1-85345-339-7

Ruth
Loving kindness in action
ISBN: 978-1-85345-231-4

The Covenants
God's promises and their relevance today
ISBN: 978-1-85345-255-0

The Divine Blueprint
God's extraordinary power in ordinary lives
ISBN: 978-1-85345-292-5

The Holy Spirit
Understanding and experiencing Him
ISBN: 978-1-85345-254-3

The Image of God
His attributes and character
ISBN: 978-1-85345-228-4

The Kingdom
Studies from Matthew's Gospel
ISBN: 978-1-85345-251-2

The Letter to the Colossians
In Christ alone
ISBN: 978-1-85345-405-9

The Letter to the Romans
Good news for everyone
ISBN: 978-1-85345-250-5

The Lord's Prayer
Praying Jesus' way
ISBN: 978-1-85345-460-8

The Prodigal Son
Amazing grace
ISBN: 978-1-85345-412-7

The Second Coming
Living in the light of Jesus' return
ISBN: 978-1-85345-422-6

The Sermon on the Mount
Life within the new covenant
ISBN: 978-1-85345-370-0

The Tabernacle
Entering into God's presence
ISBN: 978-1-85345-230-7

The Ten Commandments
Living God's Way
ISBN: 978-1-85345-593-3

The Uniqueness of our Faith
What makes Christianity distinctive?
ISBN: 978-1-85345-232-1

For current prices or to order visit www.cwr.org.uk/store
Available online or from Christian bookshops.

ver to Cover Every Day
ain deeper knowledge of the Bible

Each issue of these bimonthly daily Bible-reading notes gives
you insightful commentary on a book of the Old and New
Testaments with reflections on a psalm each weekend by
Philip Greenslade.

Enjoy contributions from two well-known authors every
two months, and over a five-year period you will be taken
through the entire Bible.

Only £2.85 each (plus p&p)
£15.50 for UK annual subscription (bimonthly, p&p included)
£13.80 for annual email subscription
(available from www.cwr.org.uk/store)

 **Individual issues available
in epub/Kindle formats**